TABLE OF CONTENTS

What Is Plagiarism?

You're ready to start working on a research paper about your favorite subject: tornadoes. You can't wait to learn new things about the windy topic! As you dive into your sources, you stumble upon the perfect way to describe a deadly tornado. The author says exactly what you want to say. You might be tempted to use those same words in your paper. After all, it's only words. Right?

Think again! Copying someone else's ideas or words and pretending they are your own is cheating. It's like stealing someone's iPod or bike. There is a specific word for stealing someone's words or thoughts: plagiarism.

Know the Rules

According to Plagiarism.org, the following are considered plagiarism:

- passing off someone else's work as your own
- copying words or ideas from someone else without giving credit
- failing to put a quotation in quotation marks
- giving incorrect information about the source of a quotation
- changing words but copying the sentence structure of a source without giving credit
- copying so many words or ideas from a source that it makes up most of your work, whether you give credit or not

quotation—text taken word for word from a book, speech, or other work; quotations are set off by quotation marks

Why Is Plagiarism a Big Deal?

Just like any type of cheating, plagiarism is a big deal. Authors, musicians, scientists, and inventors spend a lot of time writing, researching, and perfecting their craft. Many have earned advanced college degrees over years of hard work. Some have dedicated their whole lives to being the best in their fields.

Imagine you've spent years researching the migration patterns of Magellanic penguins living in South America. You've visited Chile to observe them in their natural habitat. You've recorded your observations and written a lengthy paper on the penguins. How would you feel if someone copied part of your research and pretended it was his or her idea? It wouldn't feel very good. You would probably feel angry that you hadn't been given credit for your work.

Plagiarism is a big deal on a smaller scale too. Imagine that you write a paper on Benjamin Franklin for your fourth grade history class. Three years later, your little brother has the same assignment. If he copies parts of your paper to use for his own assignment, that's plagiarism too.

Protected by Law

A person can protect his or her work by registering it with the U.S. government through copyright, trademark, or patents. Copyright protects written works, such as books or short stories, as well as works of art, film, and music. Trademarks protect brand names, symbols, and company or product logos, such as the Coca-Cola symbol. Patents protect inventions and product designs, such as the unique shape of a shoe or car.

copyright—the legal right to use, copy, or sell a book, song, or other work that others must get permission to use

trademark—a symbol that shows a product is made by a particular company

patent—a legal document giving someone sole rights to make or sell an item

It is illegal for anyone to copy a work that has been copyrighted, trademarked, or patented. Copyright laws do not protect facts or information. But they do protect the way the facts are expressed. Someone who violates the law can be taken to court.

Public Domain

Some works once protected by copyright laws have fallen into the realm of public domain. Public domain begins 75 years after the death of the creator of the work. That means the works can be used freely without risk of prosecution. But that doesn't mean you can start telling people you wrote *The Wizard of Oz*. You must still cite sources properly if you use something in the public domain.

cite—to give credit to the author of a book, short story, or other creative work, including interviews, videos, and other spoken words

JAYSON BLAIR

Jayson Blair was a journalist who wrote for *The New York Times*. Starting in 1999, Blair wrote more than 600 articles over four years. Reporters often travel to distant places and interview hundreds of people. Blair claimed to have traveled to Texas, Maryland, and other places to investigate stories. In May 2003 Blair's supervisors discovered he had been lying. He plagiarized an article from the *San Antonio Express-News* about an American soldier missing in Iraq. Instead of traveling or talking to sources on the phone, Blair plagiarized other newspapers to quote people he didn't actually interview. Deeply embarrassed, he left his job. The Blair plagiarism scandal was a disappointment to *The New York Times*—a newspaper highly respected for its accuracy. As a result, the paper added strict fact-checking policies for reporters and editors.

Jayson Blair

Research another famous case about plagiarism. Write a short paragraph about the case, including who plagiarized, what was plagiarized, and what the consequences were. Tell your teacher about what you found.

CHAPTER TWO

Citing Sources

Avoiding plagiarism does not mean you need to avoid using the words or thoughts of others. However, if you use an idea that is not your own, you must tell the reader where you found it. Don't be afraid to cite all your sources. Telling the reader the source of your information makes you look like a credible researcher.

With a proper citation, the reader should be able to find and read the original source. In fact, a thorough bibliography gives the reader a list of places to go for his or her own research on the topic.

Select Bibliography

"A Historic Week of Civil Strife." *Life*. 7 Oct. 1957. 25 March 2011. http://books.google.com/books?id=ZFYE AAAAMBAJ&pg=PA48&dq=little+rock+nine&hl=en& ei=iMaMTaeRCoWitgf-t6WgDQ&sa=X&oi=book_resu lt&ct=result&resnum=3&ved=0CDUQ6AEwAg#v=one page&q=little%20rock%20nine&f=false

"Civil rights pioneer uses pain of past to send message today." CNN. 18 May 2004. http://articles.cnn. com/2004-05-17/justice/eckford.profile_1_black-students-white-students-elizabeth-eckford?_ s=PM:LAW

Counts, I. Wilmer. *A Life Is More Than a Moment: The Desegregation of Little Rock's Central High*. Bloomington: Indiana University Press, 1999.

"Crisis in Little Rock." American Radio Works. http:// american radioworks.publicradio.org/features/ marshall/littlerock1.html

The Encyclopedia of Arkansas History & Culture Project. www.encyclopediaofarkansas.net

McWhorter, Diane. *Carry Me Home: Birmingham, Alabama: The Climactic Battle of the Civil Rights Revolution*. New York: Simon & Schuster, 2001.

Roberts, Gene, and Hank Klibanoff. *The Race Beat: The Press, The Civil Rights Struggle and the Awakening of a Nation*. New York: Alfred A. Knopf, 2006.

"Showdown in Little Rock." U.S. History.org. www.ushistory.org/us/54c.asp

Southern Oral History Program interview with Daisy Bates. 11 Oct. 1976. University of North Carolina at Chapel Hill. http://dc.lib.unc.edu/cdm4/item_viewer. php?CISOROOT=/sohp&CISOPTR=648&CISOBOX= 1&REC=1

Transcripts. Civil Rights and the Press Symposium. Oral history interviews. S.I. Newhouse School of Public Communications, Syracuse University. http:// civilrightsandthepress.syr.edu/oral_histories.html

Citing Properly

When citing a book in your research, there are four pieces of information you should always include:

- the author's name
- the title
- the publisher
- the date the document was published

After the text you're referencing, add a footnote or simply include the author's name in parentheses.

Another easy way to cite is by using the author's name in the actual sentence. For example: "According to Veronique Greenwood of *Time* magazine, there are about 40,000 species of plants in the Amazon rain forest." That's it—by recognizing the author, you've avoided plagiarism. In your bibliography, you'll include the full citation.

bibliography—an alphabetical list of the sources used in a research paper or project
footnote—a citation at the bottom of the page or at the end of a document referring to a specific section of text

Citation Guidelines

Here are the three most common styles for citation:

1 American Psychological Association (APA)—used mostly in the social sciences (psychology, sociology), business, and nursing

2 Modern Language Association (MLA)—used mostly in the liberal arts and humanities (literature, history, philosophy)

3 Chicago Manual of Style (CMS)—used mostly in literature, history, and the arts

Each style guide has a slightly different way of citing sources. All provide the same information. If your teacher doesn't recommend a style to use, be sure to stay consistent in the way you cite sources.

Citation Styles

For more information about the various styles of citation, go to the Online Writing Lab at Purdue University website (http://owl.english.purdue.edu/).

For example, this book would be cited in the following ways:

✓ **APA (6th edition):** Asselin, K. C. (2013). *Think for Yourself: Avoiding Plagiarism.* North Mankato, MN: Capstone Press.

✓ **MLA (7th edition):** Asselin, Kristine Carlson. *Think for Yourself: Avoiding Plagiarism.* North Mankato, MN: Capstone Press, 2013. Print.

✓ **CMS:** Asselin, Kristine Carlson. *Think for Yourself: Avoiding Plagiarism.* North Mankato, MN: Capstone Press, 2013.

Key:

    Author Name   Title

    Publication Year   Publication City

    Publication Company

PRACTICE EXERCISE

Pick out your favorite book and write down the author's name, the title, the publishing company's name and location, and the year. Then create the citation for the book using APA, MLA, and CMS styles.

Staying Organized

Through the research process, you'll collect many pieces of information. Organize the facts for your project in a way that will help you keep track of the information and the source. You might use note cards to write down each fact and the source where you found it. You might keep track in a computer document or in a notebook. However you organize your facts, remember to always list the source with the fact. When you're ready to write, you'll have all the information in one place.

Now you know how to cite a book, but there are more than just books for you to use! Other types of sources need to be cited in certain ways too.

Magazine, Journal, or Newspaper Articles: Articles (either online or in print) are cited similarly to books. Key pieces of information to include are the author's name, the title of the article, the magazine, journal, or periodical in which it's printed, and the date and year of publication.

The following information is from an online article about Jayson Blair. To make the citation easier, list the information you'll need.

Authors: Francois Bringer, Rose Arce
Title: New York Times Executives Apologize for Mistakes in Blair Scandal
Source: CNN, <http://articles.cnn.com/2003-05-15/us/ times.meeting_1_jayson-blair-gerald-boyd-howell-raines?_s=PM:US>
Date published: May 15, 2003
Date accessed: November 8, 2012

From the information in the list, let's create the citation using MLA style:
Bringer, Francois, and Rose Arce. New York Times Executives Apologize for Mistakes in Blair Scandal. CNN. 8 Nov. 2003. Web. 23 Aug. 2012. <http://articles.cnn. com/2003-05-15/us/times.meeting_1_jayson-blair-gerald-boyd-howell-raines?_s=PM:US>

The Internet: There are millions of words and ideas available on the Internet with the click of a mouse. With so much information at your fingertips, you can imagine how easy it is to plagiarize. Sometimes it may be hard to tell who the writer is or how to cite the source. You might think that it's not a big deal or that it's easier to skip the citations. But even if it's easy, it's still wrong to copy words or thoughts and use them as your own. It's important to take the time to cite correctly.

You should always cite the source when you use an Internet resource. Include the name of the website, the title of the article, the author, the date it was published, the date you viewed the article, and the URL address. Not all of this information may be available or appear on the website. If you can't find some of the information, be sure to at least include the name of the website, the date you retrieved the information, and the URL. This is an example of a website citation:

"What is Plagiarism?" Plagiarism.org. Accessed November 8, 2012. <http://www.plagiarism.org/learning_center/what_is_plagiarism.html>

To URL or Not to URL?

Some style guides leave out the URL for an online citation. The URLs listed might not work after awhile because they often change. Check to see if the style guide you're using includes the URL for websites and online articles.

URL—an address of a website found on the Internet

Pictures and Images: You might find a picture or image you'd like to use in your report. The same rules on plagiarism apply. If you didn't take the picture, you should cite the photographer or artist. If you don't know the name of the photographer or the artist, you should cite the source where you found the image. Book publishers have to cite their images too—check out page 2 for the photo credits!

George Washington crossing the Potomac River

Maps: If you use information from a map, you must cite the source. You'll need to include the author's name, the book or magazine, the scale, the date of publication, and the publisher. If you can't find some of the information, include as much as you can.

CHAPTER THREE

Paraphrasing and Quotations

Even when you cite the source, you should not copy someone else's exact words. You're bound to use some of the same words, but you should **paraphrase** it in your own style of writing. For example, for your project on tornadoes you might read a book about how tornadoes form. By paraphrasing the material, you can select the most important pieces of information from all your sources and write your paper in your own words.

paraphrase—to describe a fact or express someone else's thoughts using your own words

PRACTICE EXERCISE

Read the following passage about hibernation and paraphrase using your own words.

Before hibernation, animals eat more food than usual. They gain weight and store the added energy as body fat. As the temperature drops, they seek shelter in caves, burrows, or dens. Then they fall into the deep sleep of hibernation.

During this period, an animal's breathing and body functions slow down. Some hibernating animals awaken for brief periods during winter, but others have almost no activity for months. The animals emerge from hibernation when the temperatures warm up in spring.

Martin Luther King Jr.

Using Quotations

In certain situations you might need to use someone's exact words to make a particularly strong point. Use quotation marks around the phrase and give the author credit. For example, you might want to quote Martin Luther King Jr. in a project about civil rights. On August 28, 1963, he said, "I have a dream that my four little children will one day live in a nation where they will not be judged by the color of their skin, but by the content of their character." The beginning of his speech is so well known that you might want to quote it instead of paraphrase it. But don't stop there! Be sure to add your own thoughts on what the quote means to you.

COMMON KNOWLEDGE

If something is common knowledge, you don't have to cite the source. Examples of common knowledge are well-known facts, such as Earth is a planet in the solar system and there are 365 days in a year. If you are not sure if something is considered common knowledge, it's safer to find a source to confirm the fact and cite it.

CHAPTER FOUR

Avoid Plagiarism, Avoid the Consequences

Before the days of computer access and Internet technology, it was harder for teachers to tell if someone was plagiarizing. Unless the teacher was familiar with the original source, the student often got away with it. Today most teachers have access to plagiarism detection services and databases. A teacher can type a passage of your work in the search engine. If the words match a passage from another text, the teacher will know it's been plagiarized.

Search engines are great for finding information about your topic, but be sure to write about it in your own words!

Teachers are using Internet databases to crack down on plagiarism.

It might seem easy to plagiarize, but the consequences can be rough. At the very least, the plagiarist loses the respect and trust of teachers and peers. For students, consequences might range from receiving a failing grade on the project to being expelled from school. If someone earns money from copyrighted material, he or she could face a fine of up to $250,000 and 10 years in jail.

Do It Right

Though it might seem like a shortcut to plagiarize, it's just as easy to avoid it. As you are researching, be sure to read your sources carefully and paraphrase them in your own words. If you use the thought or opinion of someone else, give the author credit by citing the source. If you add your own opinion to something another person said, cite the original thought and then add your own opinion. By taking the extra steps to avoid plagiarism, you're being fair and honest. You'll also turn in a well-researched project that will hopefully land you a good grade!

29

GLOSSARY

bibliography (bib-lee-OG-ruh-fee)—an alphabetical list of the sources used in a research paper or project

cite (SITE)—to properly reference the words of another person

consequence (KAHN-suh-kwens)—the result of an action

consistent (kuhn-SIS-tuhnt)—sticking to the same form or style

copyright (KOP-ee-rite)—the legal right to use, copy, or sell a book, song, or other work that others must get permission to use

credible (KRED-uh-buhl)—trustworthy; worthy of being believed

footnote (FUT-noht)—a citation at the bottom of the page or at the end of a document referring to a specific section of text

logo (LOH-goh)—a symbol of a company's brand

paraphrase (PAIR-uh-freyz)—to express someone else's thoughts using your own words

patent (PAT-uhnt)—a legal document giving someone sole rights to make or sell a product

prosecution (pros-i-KYOO-shuhn)—the process of taking legal action against someone who has committed a crime

quotation—text taken word for word from a book, speech, or other work; quotations are set off by quotation marks

trademark (TREYD-mahrk)—a symbol that shows a product is made by a particular company

URL—an address of a website found on the Internet; URL stands for Uniform Resource Locator

READ MORE

Bentley, Nancy. *Don't Be a Copycat!: Write a Great Report without Plagiarizing.* Berkeley Heights, N.J.: Enslow Elementary, 2008.

Pulver, Beth, and Donald Adcock. *Organizing and Using Information.* Information Literacy Skills. Chicago: Heinemann Library, 2009.

Somervill, Barbara A. *Written Reports.* School Projects Survival Guides. Chicago: Heinemann Library, 2009.

Sonneborn, Liz. *Frequently Asked Questions about Plagiarism.* FAQ. Teen Life. New York: Rosen Pub., 2011.

INTERNET SITES

FactHound offers a safe, fun way to find Internet sites related to this book. All of the sites on FactHound have been researched by our staff.

Here's all you do:

Visit *www.facthound.com*

Type in this code: 9781429699518

Check out projects, games and lots more at
www.capstonekids.com

INDEX